Victory in the Struggle
Victory in the Christian Walk

Vince Hunley

Victory in the Struggle
Victory in the Christian Walk

This book is dedicated to

My Lord and Savior Jesus Christ Who has given me life and hope to live day by day. He has accepted me with all my flaws and has loved me unconditionally; He continues to grow me, love me, and have patience with me. He continues to stretch me and teach me that if I am breathing, I am blessed.

And to my lovely wife of 20+ years Dahynelia Hunley who has loved me will all her energy, strength, and heart. She has loved me in spite of me, and she shows me daily what LOVE in action looks like. I am beyond blessed because of you.

My little ones—Garrett and Christina. Wow! You have and continue to grow me up and teach me how to love. It is my privilege to be your Dad.

And, lastly to my parents—

*Dad (Otis) and Mother Dear
(Gwendolyn).
Thank you for giving me your very best
in everything.
No words can express the thanks for the
sacrifices you gave to me*

For the desires of the flesh are against the Spirit, and the desires of the Spirit are against the flesh, for these are opposed to each other, to keep you from doing the things you want to do.
Galatians 5:17 (ESV)

If there is no struggle, there is no progress. -Frederick Douglass

All life demands struggle. Those who have everything given to them become lazy, selfish, and insensitive to the real values of life. The very striving and hard work that we so constantly try to avoid is the major building block in the person we are today.
- Pope Paul VI

Strength and growth come only through continuous effort and struggle. - Napoleon Hill

Table of Contents

Insights from the author........................1

Chapter 1: Introduction.........................2

Chapter 2: DAY 1 - V Is for Victor, NOT Victim 3

Chapter 3: DAY 2 - I Is for Intelligence, NOT Ignorance 5

Chapter 4: DAY 3 - C Is for Courage, NOT Cowardice.....................................6

Chapter 5: DAY 4 - T Is for Triumph (Trials Won't Last Always)...................8

Chapter 6: DAY 5 - O Is for Obedience (The Key to Blessings) 9

Chapter 7: DAY 6 - R Is for Refuge, Not Retreat (A place to Regroup)...............11

Chapter 8: DAY 7 - Y Is for Yield (Allow Christ to Fight for You)...........13

ACKNOWLEDGMENT 14

Remember!!!..15

Please leave a review on Amazon.com.16

Author's Reading Wish List................17

Insights from the author

Wow!

A new journey, new experiences, new travel outside my comfort zone. Again— wow!

A published book. Not in my wildest dreams at the beginning of the year would I have thought this would happen.

Over the last several months I have been taking notes at the gym while waiting for Christina's basketball practice to be over or while riding on Bart. I have repeatedly experienced the frustration of getting inspirational thoughts and not having a pen, paper, or pad around. So, I have had to keep repeating the thoughts so I would not forget them.

After doing all this brain dumping to paper, it was time to put it all together—

to get the outline together, type up all the notes, and take my time to make sure it all made sense. I know I serve an EXCELLENT God, and I possess the desire to strive to do my very best with what He has placed in my heart.

I found myself equating this new opportunity to the Lord expanding my horizons, but letting me know that it was comparable to when a farmer begins to plant in new ground. The farmer first has to prepare the ground to receive the new seed. This means work would need to take place to break up the hard ground. I had to do the research and reading on self-publishing and look at examples for formats and styles; it was and still is a great learning experience.

I have learned much during this process about myself, my daily Christian walk, and God's faithfulness when you make the choice to persevere.

My greatest hope in putting this small

devotional together is that it will strengthen all who will take the 7-day challenge to walk in victory.

If you take the devotional slowly and allow the Lord to reveal the meaning of each letter to you personally, you will be blessed.

Chapter 1: Introduction

VICTORY - 7 Letters - Seven days

Read one letter per day to get your victory.

"I wait quietly before God, for my victory comes from him."

-Psalms 62:1

Christ said it best concerning the struggle.

For the desires of the flesh are against the Spirit, and the desires of the Spirit are against the flesh, for these are opposed to each other, to keep you from doing the things you want to do.-

Galatians 5:17 ESV

Once we accept Christ as Savior in our lives, our flesh (human nature) and the spirit WILL be at war until the Lord takes us to heaven to be with Him.

I know it is much easier to blame the many circumstances outside of us for the daily struggles that come to fight against us, but if we take Christ at His Word and make the faithful effort to view our struggles from His perspective, life then begins to simplify itself down to the root issues.

We are in a battle (struggle) between OUR flesh and the Holy Spirit.

The Flesh

My flesh is that part of me that wants to do what I want to do, when I want to do it, with whom I want to do it, how I want to do it, and I dare God to say something about it. I may not actually say those words, but what do my ACTIONS "say?"

The Holy Spirit

The Holy Spirit is the 3rd person of the Trinity. He is all powerful and desires to lead and guide us in all truth.   On to V.I.C.T.O.R.Y!

Chapter 2: DAY 1 - V Is for Victor, NOT Victim

15 For we do not have a high priest who is unable to sympathize with our weaknesses, but one who in every respect has been tempted as we are, yet without sin. 16 Let us then with confidence draw near to the throne of grace, that we may receive mercy and find grace to help in time of need.

-Hebrews 4:15-16 ESV

The Problems:
" I can't walk this Christian walk it is to hard, I am just not sure of myself"
"My past continues to prevent me from growing in the Lord, how can I change that?"

From Victim to Victor
How do you go from being a victim to a victor? It is easy really. Make the choice. Yes, it is that easy. Though the choice is

easy, it's the work that is hard. You may not have chosen to be a victim, but the choice of being a victor is 100% yours.

Picture this.

Growing up, I was always verbally abused by my peers for various reasons. Their words were hurtful, but as I got older, I chose to hold on that hurt.

So, if I chose to hold on to those words, I could also choose to let go!! I become an immediate victor once I decided that I have *all* the power to choose to get help for my recovery.

I must take the first step toward my recovery I can blame no one if I choose to remain a victim.

It's my choice to pray; it's my choice to seek counseling; it's my choice to rejoice!!!

I HAVE THE POWER TO WALK IN THE PATH OF RESTORATION.

Be a victim no more and choose to be a victor.

Additional Thoughts
When I take the stand of a victim, I am waiting for the one who hurt me to somehow come and make everything right. I can't begin to be healed until he takes some form of action to assist me in my healing.

When I take the stand of a victor, I take full responsibility for my restoration and my healing. I know that I am a child of the most high God and that nothing on this planet can prevent His power from doing a mighty work to restore, heal, and comfort me. I choose to be healed as I rely on His promises, which **no one** can prevent but me!

Chapter 3: DAY 2 - I Is for Intelligence, NOT Ignorance

Definition for Intelligence: The ability to learn or understand things or to deal with new or difficult situations.

Definition for ignorant: Lacking knowledge or information.

Scripture clearly tells us (2 Corinthians 2:11) that we are not ignorant to Satan's devices, schemes, and plans.

God has given us a great mind with great intelligence to learn in abundance (Matthew 11:29). More applied knowledge of His Word equals more applied power in our struggles.

How is that? The Bible clearly spells out the tactics the enemy will use against us because he thinks we are ignorant.

Lust of the flesh – Cravings and Desires outside the will of God.
Lust of the eyes – Greed, Discontenment;
Pride of life – Lacking Humilty,Boastful,

Questions to ask as you go through your day:
   - What pleasures opposite of Christ's are
   trying to draw me away?

   - What is my focus throughout my day? I
   control what I stare at and focus on.

   - Is the value of my identity determined by
   the amount of possessions I own?

Choose this day to no longer be a fool to the
things that try to temp you.

Additional Thoughts

I am intelligent (the ability to learn or
understand), and I have access to an almighty
God Who commands me that if I lack wisdom
to ask Him, and He will gladly shower me with
the wisdom I need (James 1:5). If I choose not
to answer the "why" questions of my sin, my
intelligence is wasted because I am not seeking
to learn from my experience. Therefore, I am
doomed to repeat it.

Chapter 4: DAY 3 - C Is for Courage, NOT Cowardice

Definition of courage: The ability to do something that frightens one. Strength in the face of pain or grief.

Where there is courage, there is the FEELING of fear.

Courage is merely making my mind to walk in faith, regardless of the FEAR.

Think of it this way—STARVE my fear and FEED my courage.

God tells me, *7 for God gave us a spirit not of fear but of power and love and self-control.*
2 Timothy 1:7 ESV

I must **CHOOSE** to walk in courage.

God tells me we are mighty men and women of valor! God empowers us to do great and wonderful things in His name.

"Now to him who is able to do far more

abundantly than all that we ask or think,
according to the power at work within us"
-Ephesians 3:20 ESV

"I learned that courage was not the absence of fear, but the triumph over it. The brave man is not he who does not feel afraid, but he who conquers that fear."

-Nelson Mandela

Questions to ask:
   -Where do I need courage today?

   -How have I seen courage lived out in others?

   -If God has not given me a spirit of fear, what is holding me back from living out courage in Him?

Additional Thoughts

Courage and fear are the opposite of the same coin. Without the presence of fear, courage has no place to thrive and grow. Courage simply means to act in spite of fear.

As a Christian, the fear of rejection and doubt are ever present as we learn to obey and trust Christ in our day-to-day walk. In addition to fear as an obstacle to courage, the other obstacle is our feelings/emotions. Our feelings/emotions, as we know, are ever present and ever changing.

Courage is something you do, not something you always feel.

Chapter 5: DAY 4 - T Is for Triumph (Trials Won't Last Always)

"Such trials show the proven character of your faith, which is much more valuable than gold that is tested by fire, even though it is passing away and will bring praise and glory and honor when Jesus Christ is revealed."

-1 Peter 1:7

"We all face storms in life. Some are more difficult than others, but we all go through trials and tribulation. That's why we have the gift of faith."

-Joyce Meyer

Unless we are tested or have trials in the struggle, how do we measure our growth and our maturity in Christ?

By nature, we may lean toward avoiding the inevitable trails that come our way, but without a trial there can be no testimony. Without a testimony, there is no victory.

Trials sent by God do not come to break us but to make us.

"A gem cannot be polished without friction,

nor a man perfected without trials."
                    -Lucius Annaeus Seneca

*"Being confident of this very thing, that he
which hath begun a good work in you will
perform until the day of Jesus Christ."*
                              -Philippians 1:6

Questions:
    -How big is the creator of the universe to
    you? Can He handle your issues?

    -Trials will not last always, if I allow Christ
    lead me through.

Chapter 6: DAY 5 - O Is for Obedience (The Key to Blessings)

"The bottom line in the Christian life is obedience, and most people don't even like the word."

-Charles Stanley

OUCH!

What is it about that word *obedience* that rubs us the wrong way?

Are we so determined to do things our way that the pride in us prevents us from seeing an obvious action to our success?

O B E Y—obey.

Maybe we need to change our perspective on the word *obey*.

"He who did not spare his own Son but gave him up for us all, how will he not also with him graciously give us all things?"

-Romans 8:32

God truly does desire to give us the best of the best in **all** things. God's best is always better than our version of what is best.

God will not change His plan of success for me, so I can choose to obey and receive the victory or disobey and be defeated!

"Obedience is the fruit of faith."
-Christina Rossetti

Questions:
  -What is my greatest obstacle to obedience to God?

  -Why is obeying God's commands so hard?

Additional Thoughts
"Now to Him who is able to do exceedingly

abundantly above all that we ask or think,

according to the power that works in us."

  -Ephesians 3:20, NKJV

If I am a believer in the promises of God, then

Ephesians 3:20 is

promising me a

much better outcome than I can even I imagine.

So basically, if I want to be independent from

God, and I am able to achieve the most very

best in my ability, it will still pale in comparison to what He is offering me. So, I have to ask myself what all am I leaving on the table when I chose to do it my way and not obey? Though we may love to do things our way, we are not stupid. Why would we say no when our God offering us abundant beyond what we can ask or think?

Please don't limit the abundance to people, places, and things.

His abundance will exceed that by far. What good does a bunch a money do you if you are broken-hearted and discouraged?

God treasures always exceed material possessions. Materials possessions are simply things to be managed they were never created to define my identity.

Chapter 7: DAY 6 - R Is for Refuge, Not Retreat (A place to Regroup)

Definition of refuge: A condition of being safe or sheltered from pursuit, danger, or trouble.

*"But I will sing of your strength; I will sing aloud of your steadfast love in the morning. For you have been to me a fortress and a **refuge** in the day of my distress"*

-Psalms 59:16

My refuge in God is a key to my victory in the struggle, for it assures me that I will always have a place of rest and safety for my emotions, mind, and spirit. When I feel I am overwhelmed with life, I can run to Christ and find my stability in Him.

What are the practical steps to finding refuge in Him?

By faith, we must believe His promise that He is a refuge (You may not always feel it, but believe what He has promised).

"Casting all your anxieties on him, because he cares for you."

-1Peter 5:7 ESV

I must **give** my cares to Him; He will not snatch them from me.

Talk to Christ from your heart, the most self-protected part of you.

How transparent have I allowed myself to be with Christ?

"God is our refuge and strength, a very present help in trouble"
                                                    -Psalms 46:1ESV

"For as the heavens are higher than the earth, so are my ways higher than your ways and my thoughts than your thoughts"
                                                    -Isaiah 55:9 ESV

Additional Thoughts

Wow. Technology. How did we survive without smart-phones, voicemail, email, and the list goes on and on? Information overload.

How is it working out being "connected" 24/7?

All the dings, the beeps, the alerts day after day.

Don't get me wrong; I love technology. I have

been in the computer field for 20+ years and see

that the tool of technology can make life management great when used wisely.

But (Yes, there is a but!) . . .

It is great to have a refuge to become "disconnected" and instead surrounded by peace and quiet—to clearly here the Lord's voice.

That is what a refuge is to me—a place of mental restoration and connection with Christ, so that I can manage and face all the busyness that simply comes along with leading a responsible and intentional lifestyle.

Chapter 8: DAY 7 - Y Is for Yield (Allow Christ to Fight for You)

"And no creature is hidden from God, but everything is naked and exposed to the eyes of him to whom we must render an account.
-Hebrews 4:13

When you're driving on the street and come to an intersection after another driver is already there, why do you yield? Most of the time there is no policeman watching us. We yield by choice.

It is no different with Christ. Either He has done a work in our lives to where we have come to experience the success of yielding to Him, or we are still considering yielding.

Let's keep it simple. There can only be **one** head and one authority. As we know, anything with more than one head is considered a monster and unnatural.

The principle of Exodus 20:3 ESV still applies, "You shall will have no other God before me." God will not allow anything or anyone to replace Him on the throne of your life as a Christian.

Yes, it is a tug of war for ownership.

1 Corinthians 6:20 tells us that we were bought with a price, so we must honor God with our bodies. It sounds like every time we try to take back ownership, we fall into a wrestling match with God.

"Humble yourselves, therefore, under the mighty hand of God so that at the proper time he may exalt you" -
-1 Peter 5:6

Spoiler Alert: Yield now, for you cannot win this one!

No, I did not say you would feel like yielding. You must weigh the pain of staying on the throne of your life with the blessings of relinquishing control.

Ephesians 3:20 tells us that He will do exceeding and abundantly above all I could ask or think according to the power that works in me.

If we don't yield, His power can't work and we are stuck with mediocre choices.

Yield and allow (He won't force you!) Christ to fight and work in your life.

VICTORY is through Christ. Don't be the obstacle to His blessings.

ACKNOWLEDGMENT

I would like to acknowledge my family at The Living Word Community Church in Oakland, CA. I remember praying to the Lord 23 years ago to help me find a church that taught the practical application of the Word of God. I desired a genuine walk and RELATIONSHIP with the Lord, not a religion. To me, religion is when I am trying to move towards God with all my actions to validate who I am, whereas a relationship is yielding and allowing the Lord to come into my life to make me and mold me into His Son Christ, knowing that I am defined by my relationship with Christ, not by the works I perform. I perform my works because of WHO I am (a child of the most high God) NOT to DEFINE who I am.

Thank you, Living Word Community Church family, for your love throughout the years.

Remember!!!

V is for victor (in Christ's power).

I is for intelligence (We are not ignorant to Satan's devices.).

C is for courage (Fear will not win!).

T is for triumph (Trials don't last always.).

O is for obedience (the key to my blessings).

R is for refuge (a place to regroup for the battle).

Y is for yield (Allow Christ to fight our battles.).

Please leave a review on Amazon.com.

Your feedback is important to me.

Thank you for taking the time to read through *Victory in the Struggle*.

Please go to Amazon and leave an honest review. Any and all feedback is appreciated.

Star Ratings:
1 star - Poor
2 stars - Fair
3 stars - Average
4 stars - Good
5 stars – Excellent

Author's Reading Wish List

Thinking for a Change: 11 Ways Highly
Successful People Approach Life and Word

The 17 Indisputable Laws of Teamwork

Falling Forward: Turning Mistakes into Stepping
Stones

Developing the Leader Within You

Maxwell Leadership Bible

The Exemplary Husband - A Biblical
Perspective

The Case for a Creator

Love, Sex and Lasting Relationships

Coming in 2015

16440843R00023

Made in the USA
San Bernardino, CA
03 November 2014